FRANZ LISZT

Complete Etudes for Solo Piano

SERIES II

Including the Paganini Etudes and Concert Etudes

Edited by Ferruccio Busoni

DOVER PUBLICATIONS, INC., *New York*

This Dover edition, first published in 1988, is a republication of a portion of Vol. 2 and all of Vol. 3 (both titled *Etüden für Pianoforte zu zwei Händen*) of Ser. 2 (*Pianofortewerke*) of the set *Franz Liszt's Musikalische Werke herausgegeben von der Franz Liszt-Stiftung*, originally published by Breitkopf & Härtel, Leipzig, n.d. (editor's commentaries dated 1911). A table of contents has been added, and a new translation of the editorial notes has replaced the original German.

We are grateful to the Paul Klapper Library of Queens College for the loan of the score.

Library of Congress Cataloging-in-Publication Data

Liszt, Franz, 1811–1886.
  [Etudes, piano]
  Complete etudes for solo piano.

  Reprint. Originally published: Musikalische Werke. Leipzig : Breitkopf & Härtel, 1910–1911, (Series II, v. 1–3) With translated introd.
  Contents: ser. 1. Etude en 12 exercices : op. 1, 1826 ; 12 grandes études : 1837 ; Mazeppa : 1840 ; Etudes d'exécution transcendante : 1851—ser. 2. Grande fantaisie de bravoure sur La clochette de Paganini : op. 2, 1832 ; Etudes d'exécution transcendante d'après Paganini : 1838 ; Grandes études de Paganini : — [etc.]
  1. Piano music. I. Busoni, Ferruccio, 1866–1924. II. Title.
M22.L77E83 1988   88-752979
ISBN 0-486-25815-7 (v. 1)
ISBN 0-486-25816-5 (v. 2)

Manufactured in the United States by Courier Corporation
25816510
www.doverpublications.com

Contents

Contents

Editorial Notes

Grande Fantaisie de Bravoure

Source: *Grande Fantaisie de Bravoure* sur la Clochette de Paganini, Oeuvre 2. (Vienne, Pietro Mechetti qᵐ Carlo.)

Page 6   4th staff, 4th bar. The first eighth-note of the right hand is written simply as [musical example] in the source. The lower octave has been added in accordance with the setting of the analogous passages.

" 10   3rd staff, 2nd bar. In the source a ♭ appears by the lower note in the first double note of the right hand (C♭ instead of C), but this is an engraver's error.

" 15   In the simplified version (over the 2nd bar in the 1st system), the first double note in the right hand in the source appears as [musical example], which, as an evident engraver's error, has been changed to [musical example].

" 15   Last staff: The first bar contains seven eighth-notes rather than the normal six. Whether this is the composer's or engraver's error or a rhythmic extravagance cannot be determined by the editor—especially owing to the exceptional circumstance that only the Mechetti edition of this piece exists and a comparison with other editions was thus impossible.

" 21   2nd staff, 1st bar. The source has an A as the penultimate note in the right hand, which, as an obvious engraver's error, has been changed to a B♭.

" 26   3rd staff, 2nd bar. G rather than G♯ is probably intended in the right hand (see the parallel passage 4 bars later).

" 26   6th staff, 1st bar, the same.

" 30   4th staff, 2nd bar. The dot after the first chord (quarter-note) was supplied by the editor. It may be assumed that the two preceding bars were intended as a single (9/8) bar, and that the barline between them was drawn routinely by the engraver.

In the critical review of the engraved source, Professor Otto Taubmann was of kind assistance.

Paganini Etudes, Morceau de Salon, Ab Irato, Concert Etudes

Sources: *Paganini-Etüden*, 1st edition (Haslinger).
    "   " , 2nd edition (Breitkopf & Härtel).
    Morceau de Salon ⎫ (Original editions by
    Ab-Irato   ⎬ Schlesinger).
    Trois Etudes de Concert (Original editions by Kistner).
    " " " "   (Paris edition by J. Meissonnier Fils).
    Gnomenreigen ⎫ from Lebert & Starck's
    Waldesrauschen ⎬ *Klavierschule* (original editions not located).

Notes:

Page 36   3rd staff, 2nd bar and others. The symbol ∧ over two notes is an idiosyncrasy of Liszt's. It signifies a strongly accented group of notes.

" 44   2nd staff, 1st bar. The sign ═ indicates pauses that are briefer than ⌢ (see Liszt's footnotes for the 2nd etude from the *12 Grandes Etudes*).

" 58   6th staff, 2nd bar. In the source, the second chord in the left hand appears under [musical example]. However, since the accent in the whole passage should always fall on the dissonance B♭, the chord has been moved back one note to the left.

" 70   4th staff, 2nd bar. In the source, the second 32nd-note in the left hand reads [musical example].

The lower C was deleted as an apparent engraver's error.

Page 72 The notes "imitando i Flauti" and "imitando i Corni" are Liszt's. To indicate this, the parentheses in the source have been omitted. The same case on page 118 has been treated the same way.

" 82 2nd staff, 4th bar. In the source, the right hand reads . However, since the rhythm is plainly typical for this variation, this was understood as an engraver's error and so changed to

" 84 1st staff, 4th bar. The penultimate chord in the left hand must, by analogy with the second bar of this staff, read . The source mistakenly has a B as the lowest note.

" 91 In this etude, arpeggios and scales are to be rhythmically divided by the performer (not by the listener!). The tremolo must be rapid, trill-like, and precisely measured.

" 94 1st staff, 1st bar. The change of the tremolo figure from 64th-note to 32nd-note triplets provides the measure of the accelerando, insofar as the rapidity of the tremolo should not relax.

" 100 2nd staff, 1st and 2nd bars. The obstacle to the performance of the two-hand figure lies in the dissimilar position of the sixths in the right hand. One should play with high wrists and give the upper line the semblance of a legato. (Manner of playing: *quasi glissando*.)

" 100 4th staff, 2nd bar ff. The chromatic octave passages should be played with the dynamic *sfp* $\prec$. In the longest run the pedal should be changed, perhaps in the middle.

" 100 4th staff, 2nd bar. The irregular bar construction, which is found again in the parallel passage on p. 104 (second staff), must be interpreted as a cadencelike broadening of the rhythm; we are dealing here with one of Liszt's liberties and extravagances.

" 102 5th staff, 4th bar. The trill in the left hand must be, on the analogy of all the previous trills, a semitone trill; thus not D♭–E♭ as in the source, but rather D♭–E♭♭ as amended here.

Page 115 The whole fourth etude is to be played with great rhythmic and dynamic evenness and minimal use of the pedal.

" 120 The glissandos of sixths in the second and third staves are to be played with both hands.

" 123 The "theme" is to be performed with playful ease.

" 125 In variation 3 the principal voice is in the bass.

" 125 4th staff ff. In variation 4 one plays the first four bars *piano*, the next four bars *forte*, the last eight bars *piano-crescendo* up to *fortissimo*, whose climax is to be placed on the first beat of the next variation.

" 126 2nd staff ff. Variation 5 is to be played *forte ma leggiero*.

" 129 4th staff ff. The trill in variation 10 should be at 32nd-note speed throughout.

" 148 2nd staff, 1st bar. For the lowest note of the fifth eighth-note in the right hand, the source has the engraver's error G, which has been corrected to A♭.

" 160ff. For the D-flat major etude, L. Ramann's *Liszt-Pädagogium*, 4th Series (Leipzig, Breitkopf & Härtel), provides excellent instructions, to which the reader is heartily referred. The most important of these for establishing the text are the following:

The following cadence extension and thematic introduction to the finale (written for Auguste Rennebaum in 1875, autograph in her possession) follows after the scalar run and before the return of the first theme:

NB: The theme is to be played cantabile, as is its imitation in the bass.

A version of this cadenza (Liszt's autograph [1885?], in the possession of Lina Schmalhausen) reads:

The A♮ of the third bar is to be kept in the ear as a cadential pedal point up until its move to the tonic (at ×).

Liszt also wrote out for me the following "mystically suspended" ending with large triads over the descending long six-note scale (see Mosonyi's Funeral March, page 8), which was to be used ad libitum in place of the published ending.

Performance: The tempo of the scale (left hand) should be more urgent than broad, each of its notes played with the third finger, each glissato, each half-pedaled.

Page 174   1st staff, 6th bar. In the source, the marking "Ped. ad libitum" appears in parentheses. To indicate that it is the composer's own, the parentheses have been omitted.

In preparing this edition, Prof. Otto Taubmann was of kind assistance.

Grande Fantaisie de Bravoure sur la Clochette de Paganini
Large Bravura Fantasy on Paganini's "La Campanella"
Op. 2

Variation à la Paganini.

Moderato.

*) p leggiero e sempre staccato

poco crescendo — — — — — — sf p scherzando — poco rallent

m.g.   m.g.

rfz   molto cresc.   f

Die 6/8-Schläge sind durch geschmeidiges Abheben der Hand zu markieren.
Marquez les 6 temps de la mesure en jetant la main avec souplesse.
The 6/8 time is to be marked by lifting off the hand very smoothly.

campanella

dolce   leggierissimo
egualmente
p   m.d.
pp   pp

più dolce

m.g.
poco rallentando — — — — —

*) Alle Noten mit nach unten gekehrten Stielen müssen von der linken Hand gespielt werden.
Toutes les notes dont les queues sont tournées en bas doivent être faites par la main gauche.
All the notes with the stems turned downward must be played with the left hand.

Vom Komponisten so gespielt.
Exécuté par l'Auteur.
Executed by the author.

Piano zu 6 Oktaven.
Piano à 6 octaves.
Pianoforte of 6 Octaves.

Etudes d'Exécution Transcendante d'après Paganini
Etudes for Transcendental Technique after Paganini

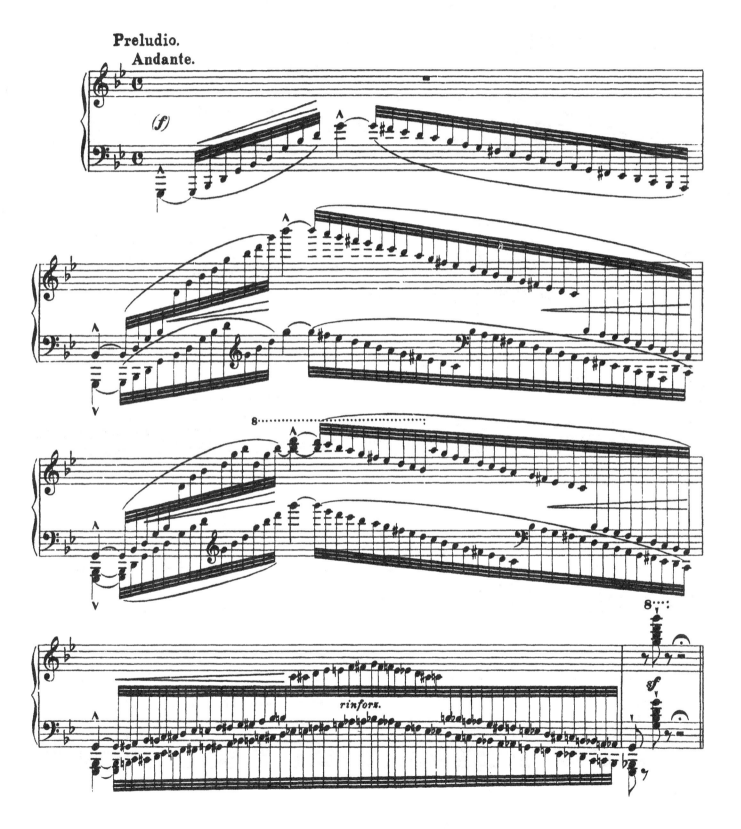

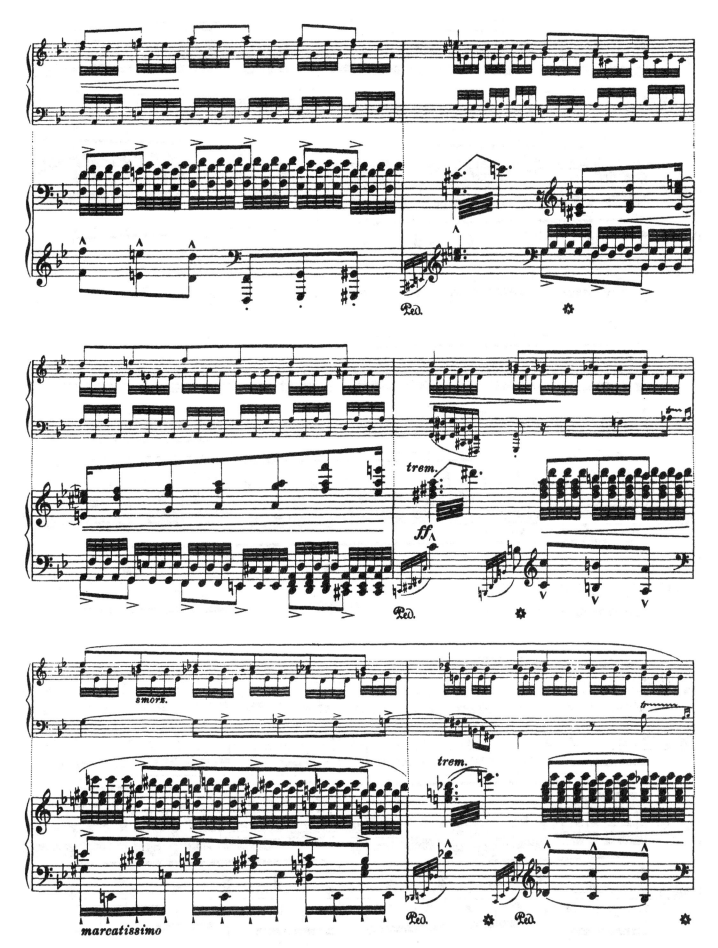

Piano zu 6 Oktaven.
Piano à 6 octaves.
Pianoforte of 6 Octaves.

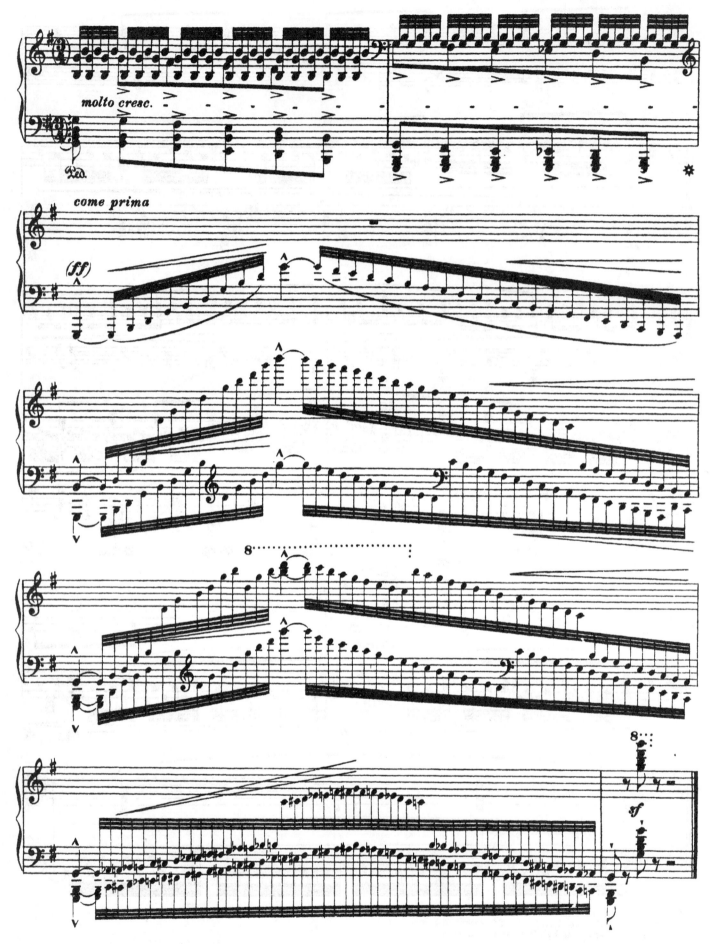

2.

44

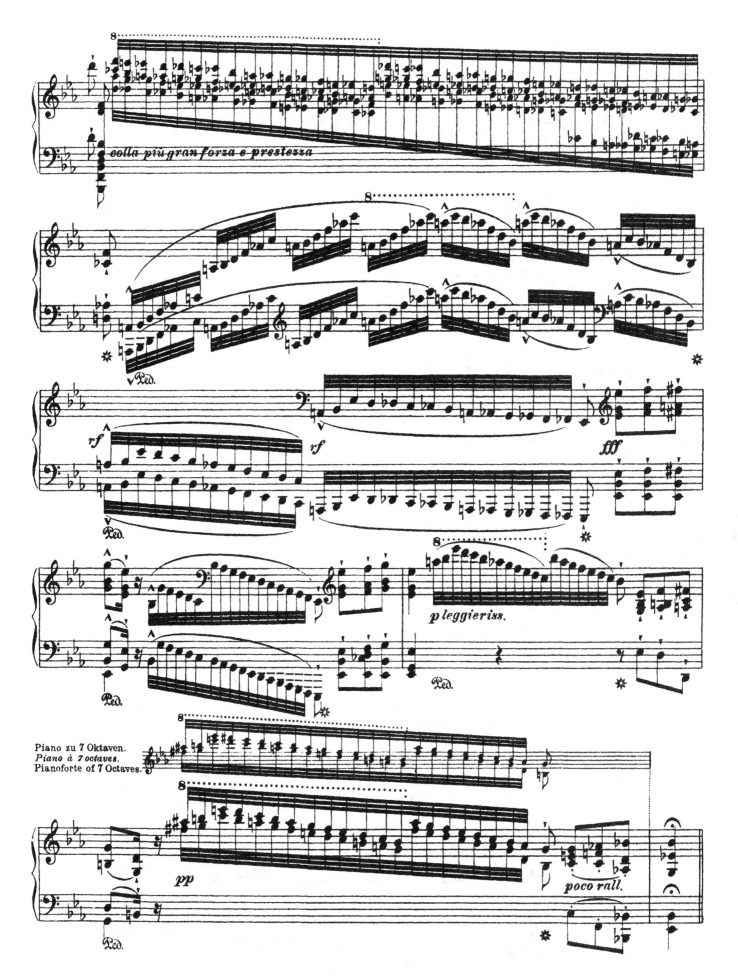

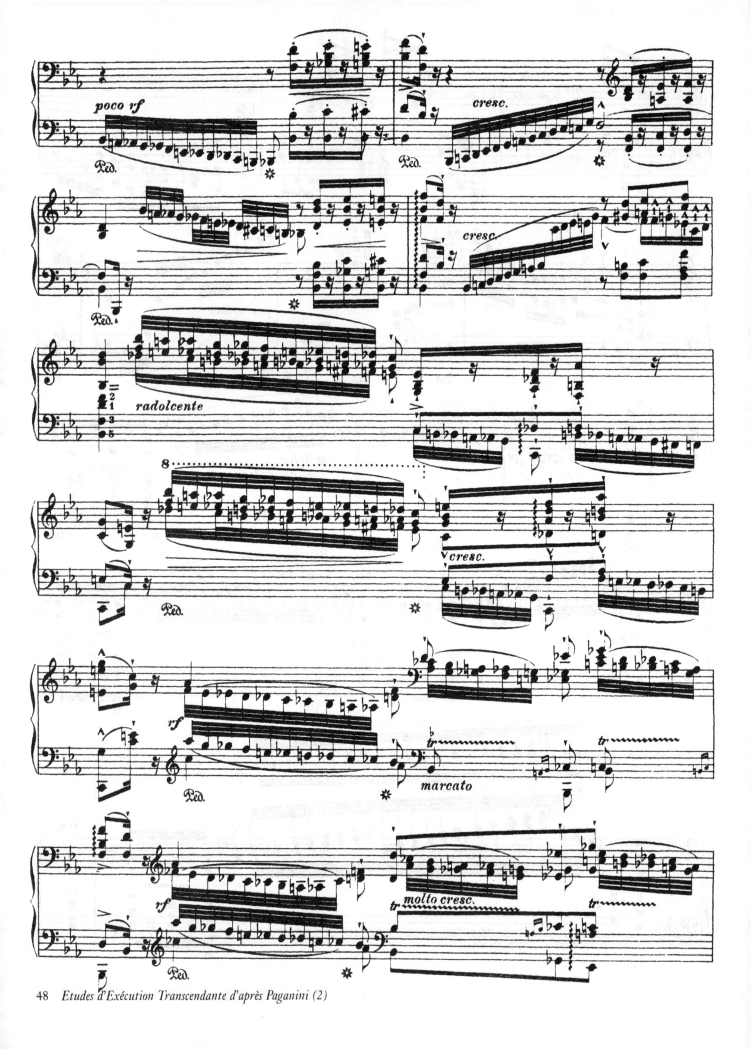

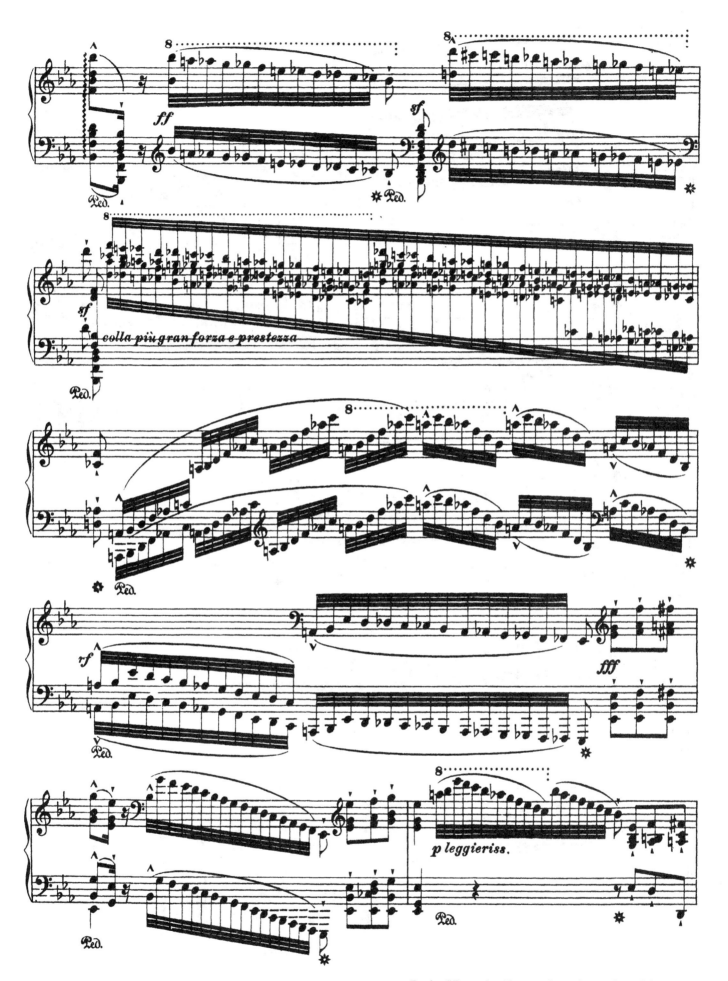

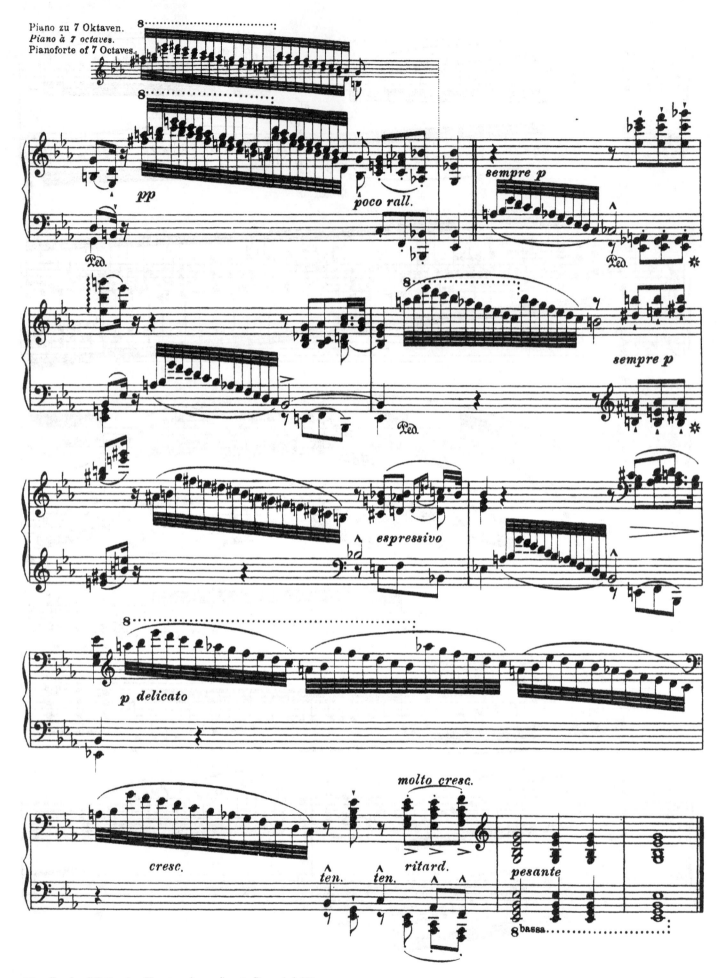

Etudes d'Exécution Transcendante d'après Paganini (2)

3.

La Campanella

Allegro moderato.

4.

(Version I)

sempre più dim.

65

Ossia

Var. II.

Etudes d'Exécution Transcendante d'après Paganini (6: Theme and Variations)

Grandes Etudes de Paganini
Paganini Etudes

1.

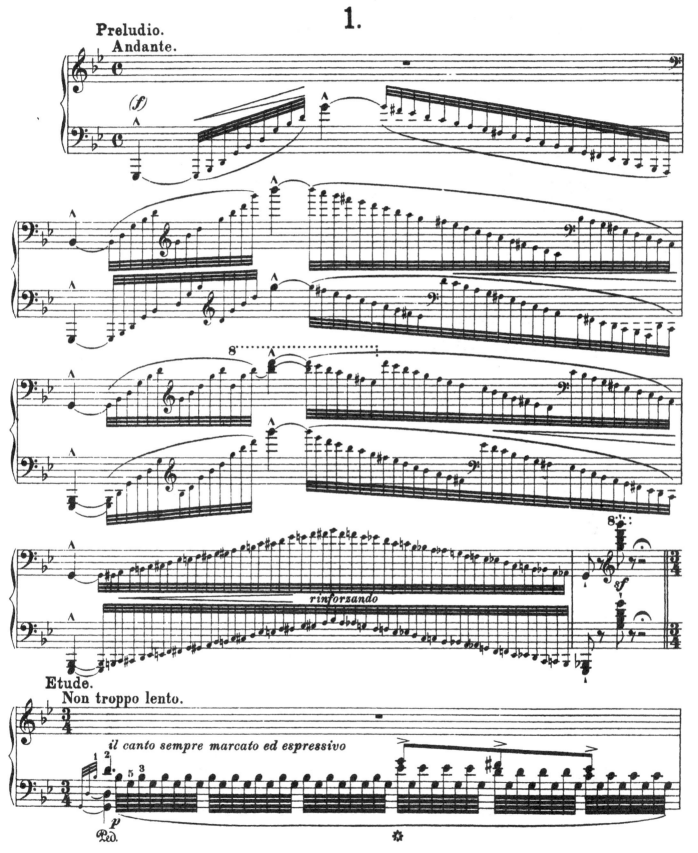

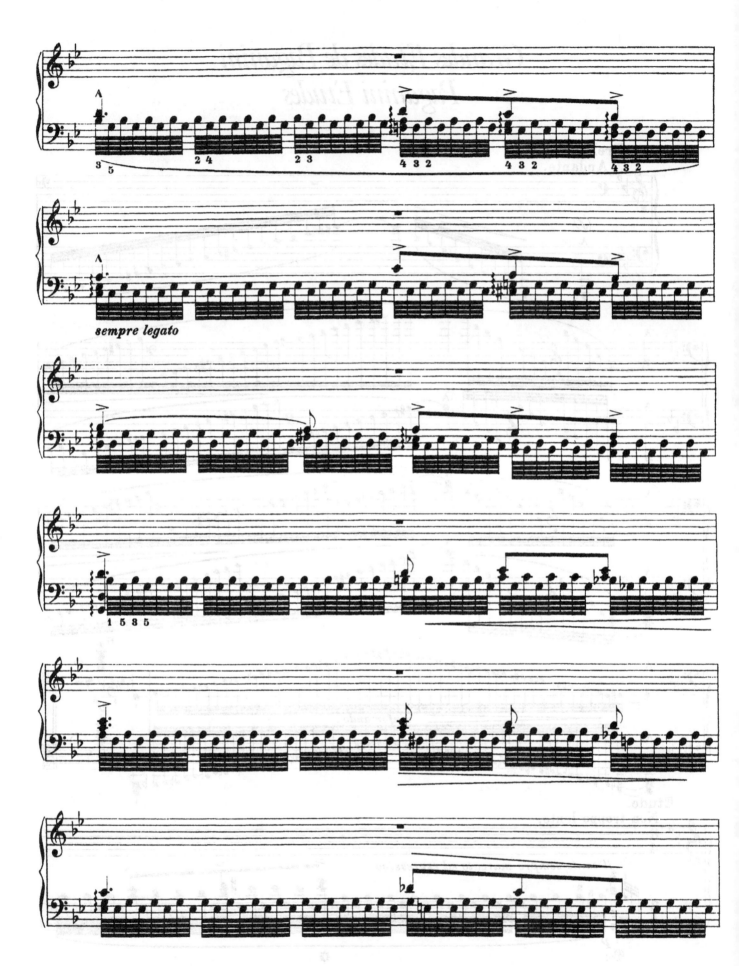

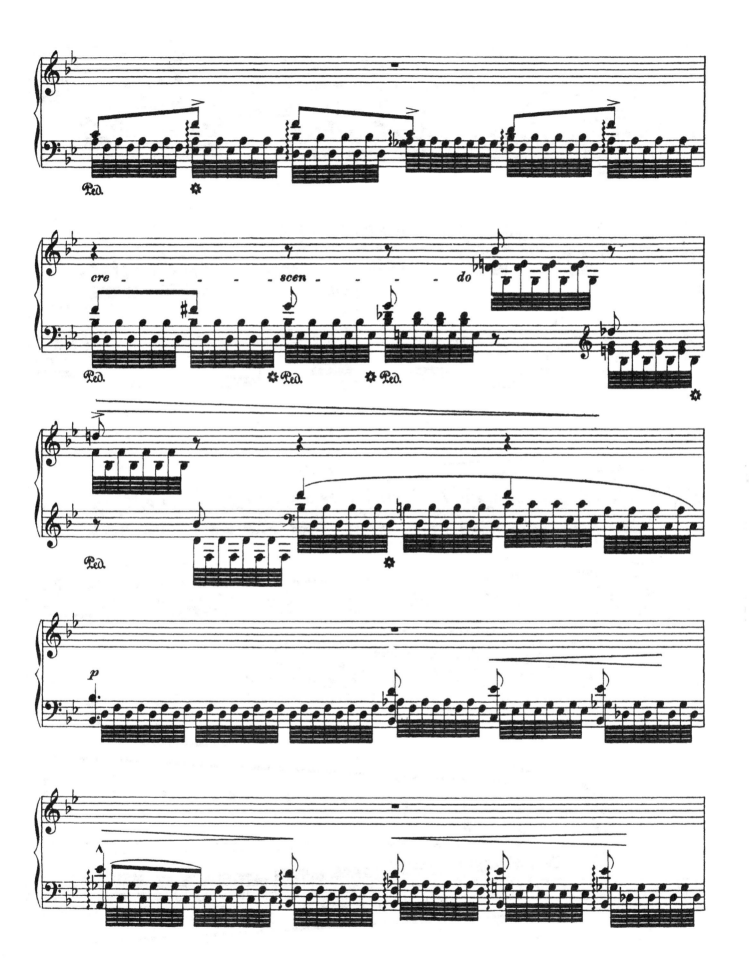

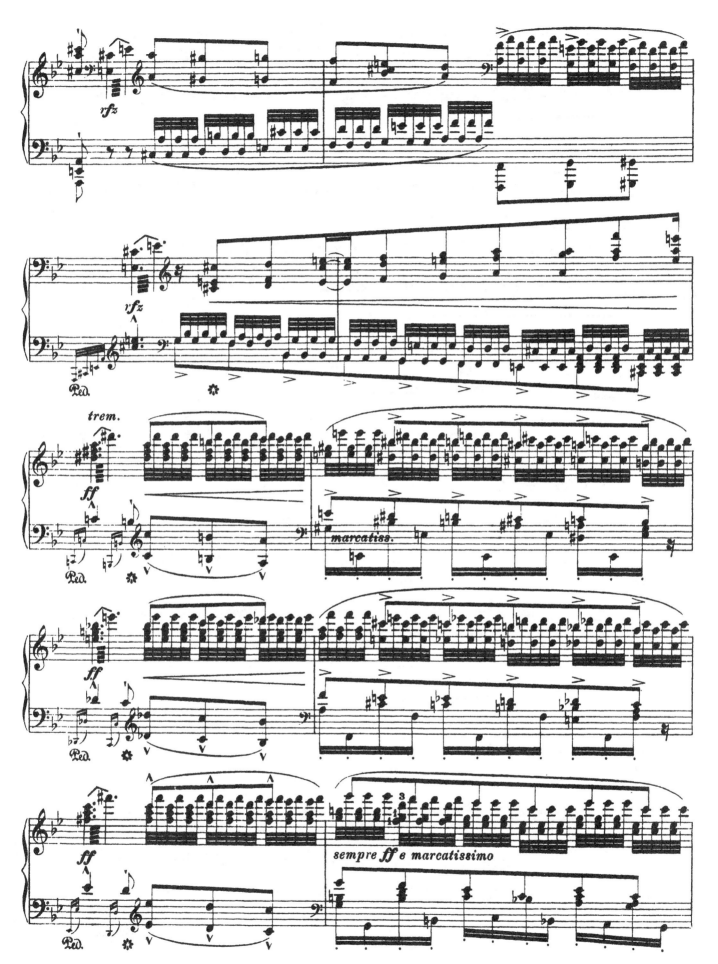

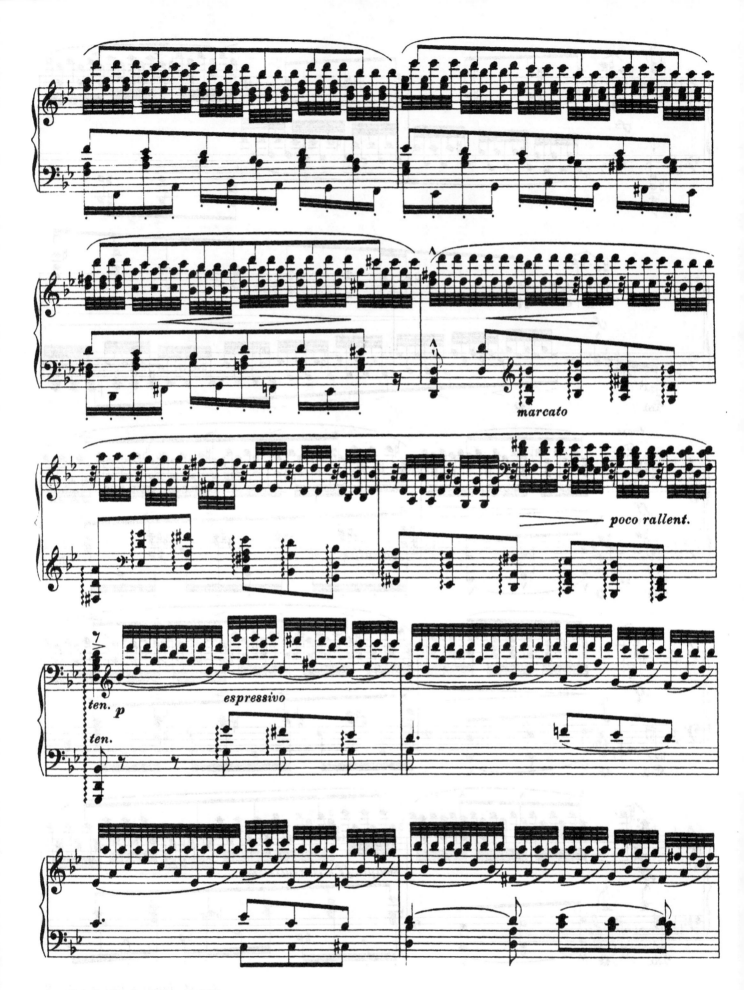

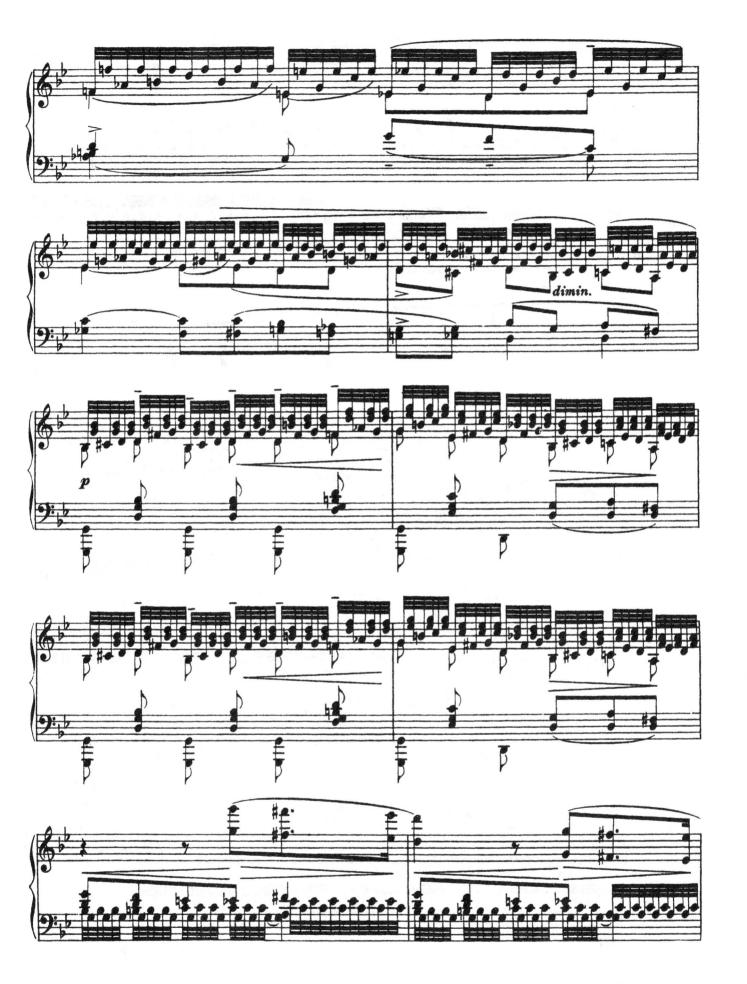

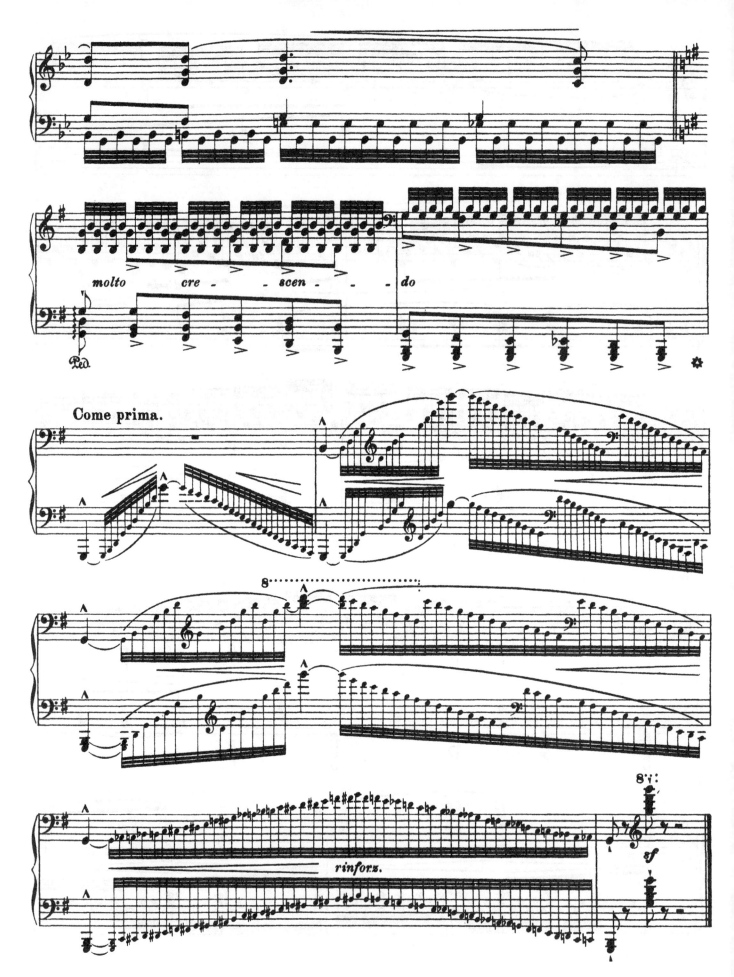

2.

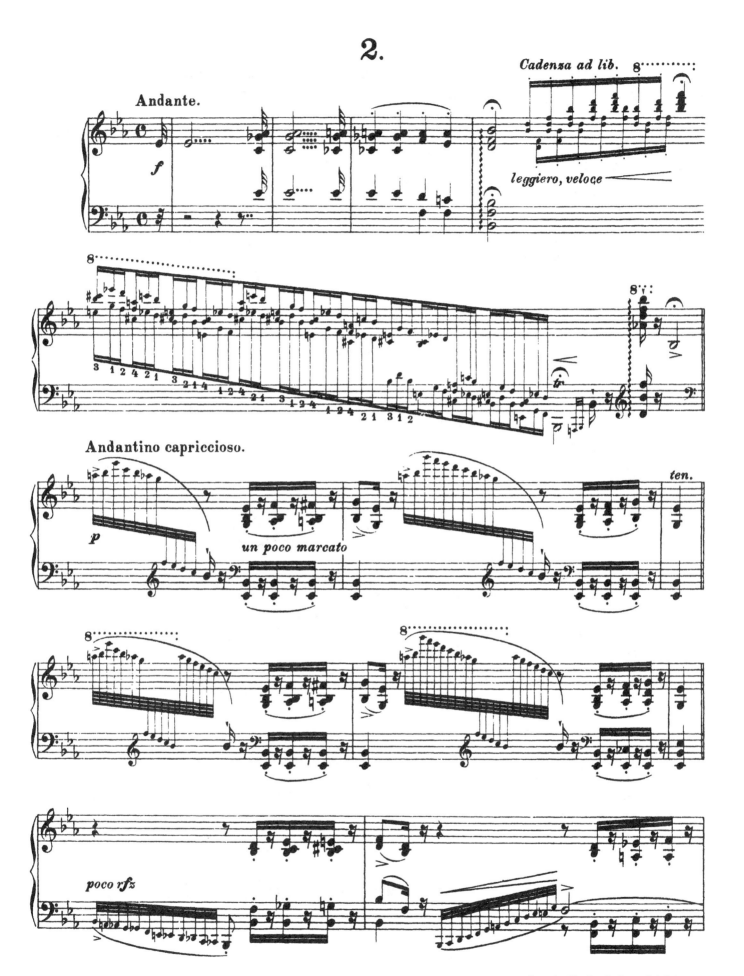

3.

La Campanella

Grandes Etudes de Paganini (3: La Campanella)

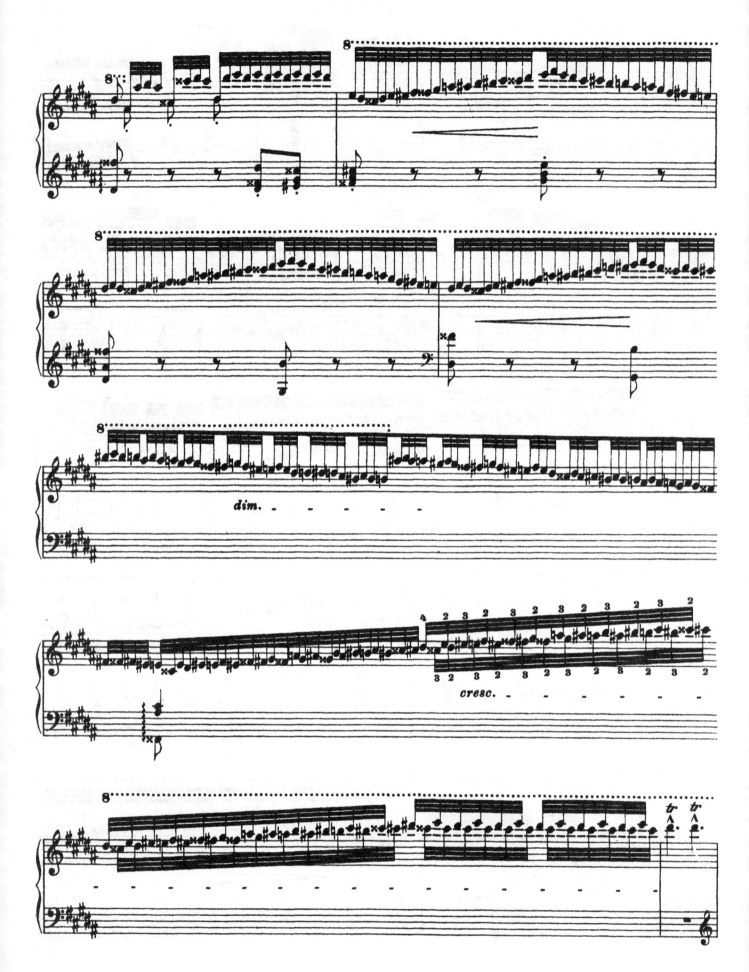

Animato.

4.

5.

Grandes Etudes de Paganini (5)

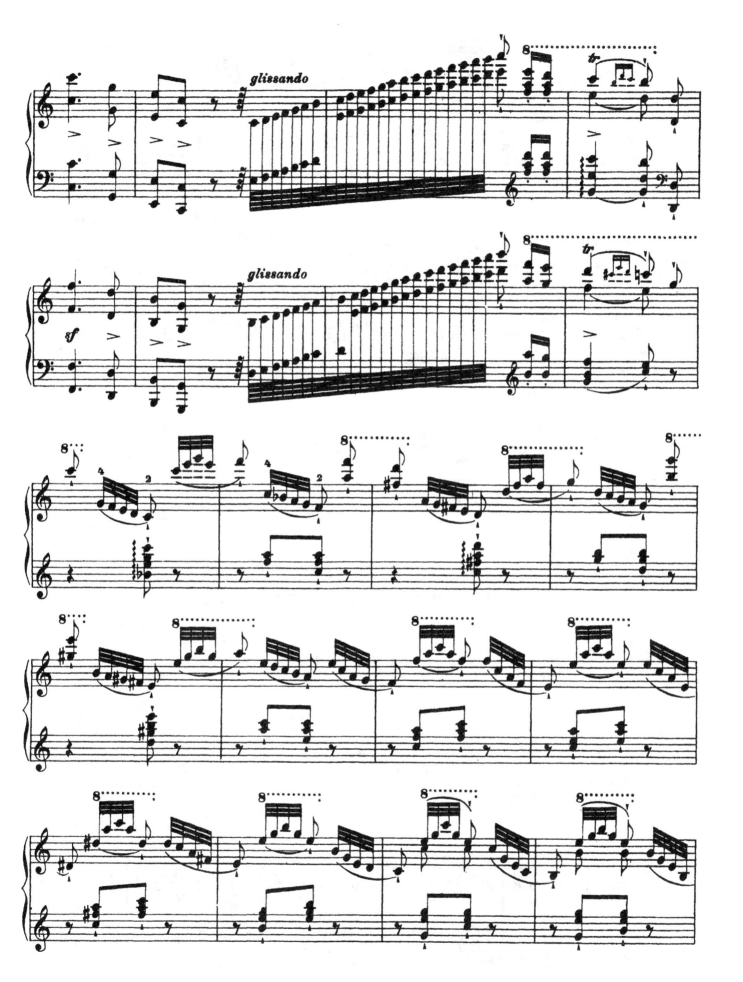

6.

Quasi Presto.

Var. 1.

Var. 2.

rit._ _ perdendosi

Morceau de Salon: Etude de Perfectionnement
Salon Piece: Finishing Etude

Ab Irato: Grande Etude de Perfectionnement
Ab Irato: Large Finishing Etude

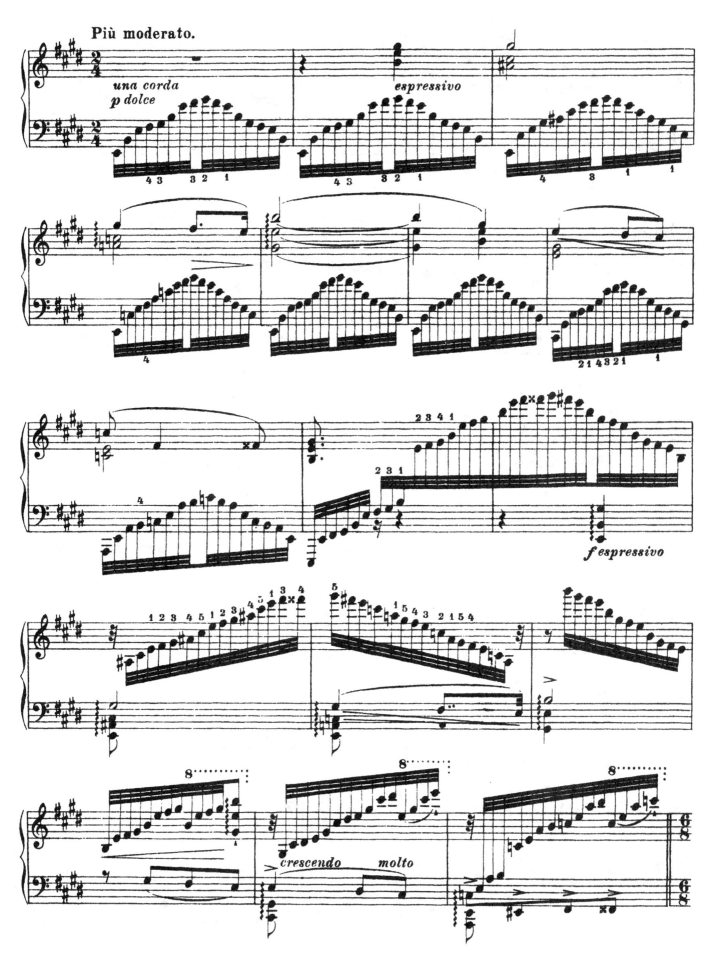

Presto agitato assai.

Trois Etudes de Concert
Three Concert Etudes

1.

2.

3.

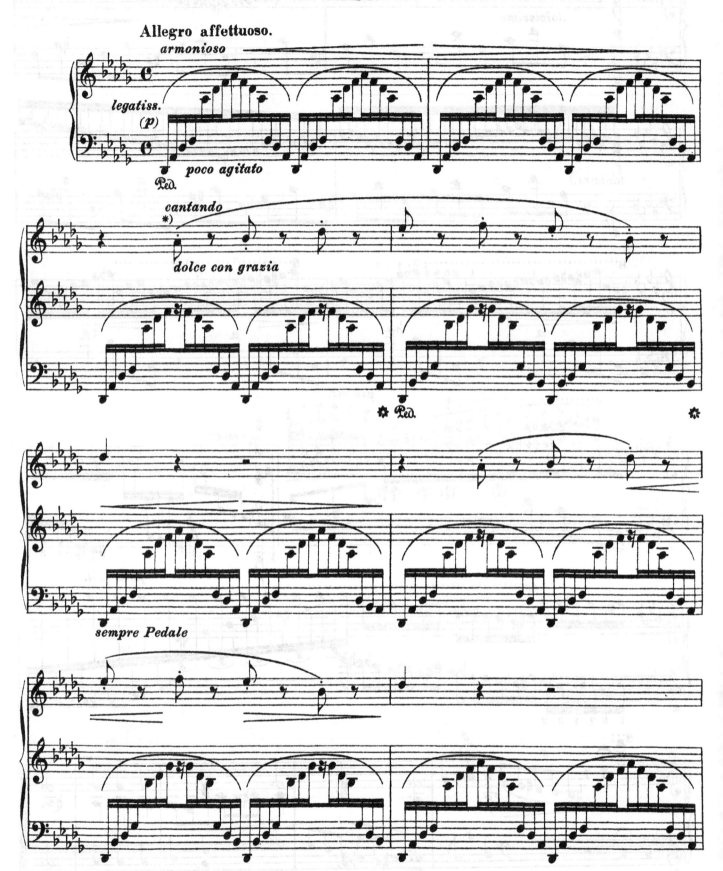

*) Die nach unten gestrichenen Noten sind mit der linken, die nach oben gestrichenen mit der rechten Hand zu spielen.
On jouera avec la main gauche les notes dont la queue est descendante, avec la droite celles dont la queue est ascendante.
The notes with stems pointing downwards are to be played with the left, those with stems pointing upwards, with the right hand.

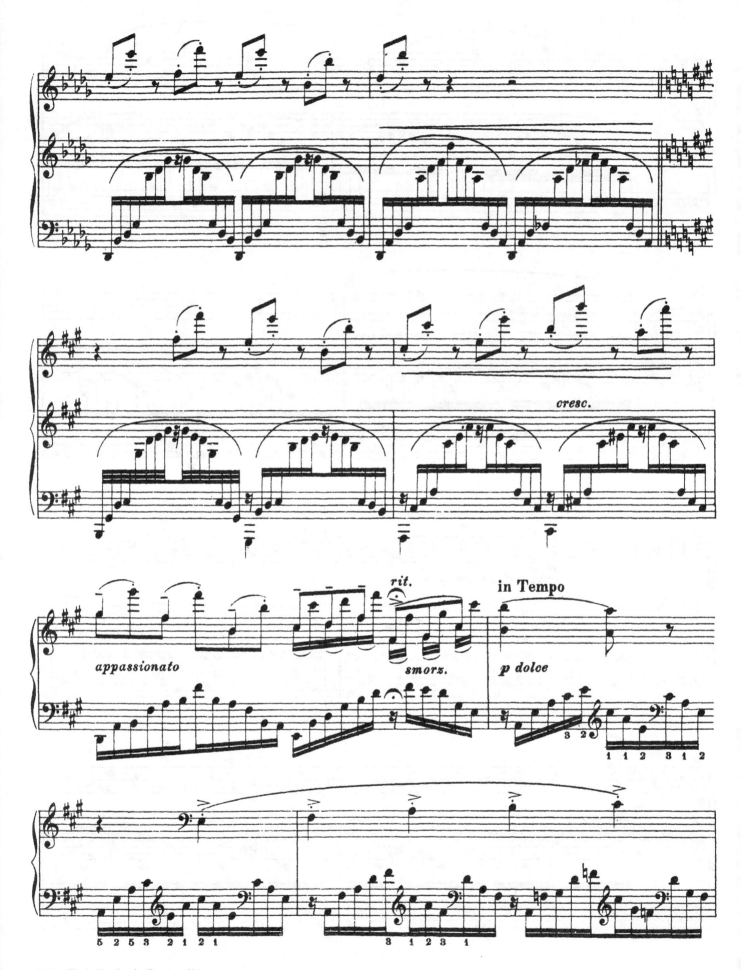

Two Concert Etudes

Gnomenreigen

Un poco più animato.

p giocoso non legato

cresc.

più cresc.

molto marcato

170   *Two Concert Etudes (Gnomenreigen)*

Waldesrauschen